MW01017539

# The Brooker's Daily Gratitude Journal

## David George Brooke
## The Brooker – That Gratitude Guy

Copyright © 2014 David George Brooke. All rights reserved. No portion of this book may be reproduced mechanically, electronically, or by any other means, including photocopying, without written permission of the publisher. It is illegal to copy this book, post it to a website, or distribute it by any other means without permission from the publisher.
David George Brooke
22722 29th Drive SE #100
Bothell, WA 98021
206-371-8309
thebrooker@thebrooker.com
http://www.thebrooker.com

**Limits of Liability and Disclaimer of Warranty**

The author and publisher shall not be liable for your misuse of this material. This book is strictly for informational and educational purposes.

**Warning – Disclaimer**

The purpose of this book is to educate and entertain. The author and/or publisher do not guarantee that anyone following these techniques, suggestions, tips, ideas, or strategies will become successful. The author and/or publisher shall have neither liability nor responsibility to anyone with respect to any loss or damage caused, or alleged to be caused, directly or indirectly by the information contained in this book.

**In case this journal is lost, please return to:**

Name: _Owen M_____

Phone#: _____

E-Mail: _____

## Dedication

To my sons Connor and Kyle, my mother Helene, and anyone looking for daily direction, inspiration, and empowerment.

# Contents

## Acknowledgements

Bob Crosetto, Katherin Scott, and many others who encouraged me to seek out the wonders of gratitude and share it's message.

Everyone needs something that can direct, inspire, and empower them to move forward every day.  There is tremendous power in living with gratitude.  This gratitude will change your life, and after all.... if you want to change your life..."change your life" Recording your gratitude thoughts and feelings will reinforce them in your mind even further.

*"If you think about it, it's like a dream,*
*If you talk about it, it inspires you, but,*
*If you write about it, it empowers you"*

*~David George Brooke*

# How to use The Brooker's Daily Gratitude Journal

## Enter the Day and Date

Write the day and date of your daily journal entry.

## Daily Number

Record your "daily number" which is between 1 and 10. Your daily number describes your current "frame of mind" and enables you to track your feelings/attitude from one day to the next. 1 is you are experiencing one of your toughest days ever, and 10 is one of the best days of your life. By tracking this all-important number, you are able to link certain daily events that can help you stay in a positive and grateful frame of mind.

## Current Events & Special Occasions

List any special event or significant occurrence that you may want to reference at a later time.

## Gratitude Today

Record the first thoughts that come into your mind. Try to consciously list items in the order of highest importance. Be aware of your health, your family, your friends, your relationships, your job, your home, and maybe just the fact you got to take a hot shower this morning.

## Gratitude Tomorrow

This is everything you are *going* to be grateful for. As your mind focuses forward, an intentioned mind will direct itself towards your future thoughts of gratitude.

## Highlight of the Day

List something that was the most memorable aspect of your day. This will help you to focus on a positive event in the past 24-hours.

GRATITUDE TODAY  Day: Wendy
Date: 3-8-2017      Daily#: 6

Current Events/Special Occasion:

I want to do DD
a feild trip fo school.

I am so Grateful for:

That my faily is not

Poor and that I can

do many fun things

The Highlight of my day was:

I am Writing this book that
in.

*Feeling gratitude and not expressing it is like wrapping a present and not*

*giving it. ~William Arthur Ward*

# GRATITUDE TOMORROW

That tomorrow I will do a good Job. on my test and it be f more Fun.

GRATITUDE TODAY Day: Thursday
Date: 3-9-2017                          Daily#: 8

Current Events/Special Occasion:
I got a brown
stripe belt.

I am so Grateful for:
That I did so good
at my test in school
and at DMW

The Highlight of my day was:
geting my brown stripe
belt.

*The single greatest thing you can do to change your life today would be to start being grateful today - Oprah Winfrey*

## GRATITUDE TOMORROW

That I will have
lots of fun on skiing
and have a fun day at
school.

GRATITUDE TODAY  Day: Sunday
                 Date: 3-12-2017          Daily#: 3

Current Events/Special Occasion:
done with my minecraft
village

I am so Grateful for:
That I have food to
eat that my mom
makes moer or dad.

The Highlight of my day was:
my minecraft village.

*Silent gratitude isn't much use to anyone. ~G.B. Stern*

## GRATITUDE TOMORROW

That I Will do

good at P.C.

**GRATITUDE TODAY** Day: Monday
Date: 13-13-17

Daily#: 5

Current Events/Special Occasion:

I made a swoosh in basketball

I am so Grateful for:

That I have my friends

by my side

The Highlight of my day was:

The swoosh in basketball.

*If the only prayer you said in your whole life was, "thank you," that would suffice. ~Meister Eckhart*

## GRATITUDE TOMORROW

That I will make a new friend that I will play with alot.

GRATITUDE TODAY   Day: Wenday
                  Date: 3-15-17                    Daily#: 5

Current Events/Special Occasion:
Made a bascet in basketball

I am so Grateful for:
That I have my dog
river.

The Highlight of my day was:
making the basket.

*There is no such thing as gratitude unexpressed. If it is unexpressed, it is plain, old-fashioned ingratitude. ~R.Brault*

## GRATITUDE TOMORROW

That I will have a
lot more fun than today.

GRATITUDE TODAY  Day: Thursday
                 Date: 3-16-2017                    Daily#:

Current Events/Special Occasion:

_____

_____

I am so Grateful for:

_____

_____

_____

_____

_____

_____

_____

_____

_____

_____

The Highlight of my day was:

_____

_____

*Gratitude is the memory of the heart. ~Jean Baptiste Massieu, translated from French*

# GRATITUDE TOMORROW

**GRATITUDE TODAY** Day: Sunday
Date: 3-26-2017    Daily#: 5

Current Events/Special Occasion:

SK ine on d bider
texy

I am so Grateful for:

my rynily dna That
The love me.

The Highlight of my day was:

eting pancakes in the
moring.

*When we were children we were grateful to those who filled our stockings at Christmas time. Why are we not grateful? ~G.K.*

## GRATITUDE TOMORROW

That School Will be
Fun

GRATITUDE TODAY   Day:
                                Date:                                    Daily#:

Current Events/Special Occasion:

_____

_____

I am so Grateful for:

_____

_____

_____

_____

_____

_____

_____

_____

_____

_____

The Highlight of my day was:

_____

_____

*The only people with whom you should try to get even are those who have helped you. ~John E. Southard*

# GRATITUDE TOMORROW

GRATITUDE TODAY  Day:
                 Date:                          Daily#:

Current Events/Special Occasion:

_____

_____

I am so Grateful for:

_____

_____

_____

_____

_____

_____

_____

_____

_____

_____

The Highlight of my day was:

_____

_____

*Gratitude is an art of painting an adversity into a lovely picture. ~Kak Sri*

# GRATITUDE TOMORROW

# GRATITUDE TODAY   Day:
Date:                                                      Daily#:

Current Events/Special Occasion:

_____

_____

I am so Grateful for:

_____

_____

_____

_____

_____

_____

_____

_____

_____

The Highlight of my day was:

_____

_____

_____

*As each day comes to us refreshed and anew, so does my gratitude renew itself daily. Terri Gauteet*

# GRATITUDE TOMORROW

GRATITUDE TODAY  Day:
                 Date:                        Daily#:

Current Events/Special Occasion:

_____

_____

I am so Grateful for:

_____

_____

_____

_____

_____

_____

_____

_____

_____

_____

The Highlight of my day was:

_____

_____

*I would maintain that thanks are the highest form of thought; and that gratitude is happiness doubled by wonder. ~G.K.*

# GRATITUDE TOMORROW

GRATITUDE TODAY   Day:
                  Date:                                    Daily#:

Current Events/Special Occasion:

_____

_____

I am so Grateful for:

_____

_____

_____

_____

_____

_____

_____

_____

_____

_____

The Highlight of my day was:

_____

_____

*If a fellow isn't thankful for what he's got, he isn't likely to be thankful for what he's going to get. ~Frank A. Clark*

# GRATITUDE TOMORROW

GRATITUDE TODAY    Day:
                                    Date:                                    Daily#:

Current Events/Special Occasion:

_____

_____

I am so Grateful for:

_____

_____

_____

_____

_____

_____

_____

_____

_____

The Highlight of my day was:

_____

_____

*The unthankful heart... discovers no mercies; but the iron, so it will find, heavenly blessings! ~Henry Ward Beech*

# GRATITUDE TOMORROW

GRATITUDE TODAY   Day:
                  Date:                           Daily#:

Current Events/Special Occasion:

_____

_____

I am so Grateful for:

_____

_____

_____

_____

_____

_____

_____

_____

_____

_____

The Highlight of my day was:

_____

_____

*Grace isn't a little prayer you chant before receiving a meal. It's a way to live. ~Attributed to Jacqueline Winspear*

# GRATITUDE TOMORROW

GRATITUDE TODAY  Day:
                 Date:                                    Daily#:

Current Events/Special Occasion:

_____

_____

I am so Grateful for:

_____

_____

_____

_____

_____

_____

_____

_____

_____

_____

_____

The Highlight of my day was:

_____

_____

*Praise the bridge that carried you over. ~George Colman*

# GRATITUDE TOMORROW

GRATITUDE TODAY   Day:
                  Date:                              Daily#:

Current Events/Special Occasion:

_____

_____

I am so Grateful for:

_____

_____

_____

_____

_____

_____

_____

_____

_____

The Highlight of my day was:

_____

_____

*If you count all your assets, you always show a profit. ~Robert Quillen*

# GRATITUDE TOMORROW

GRATITUDE TODAY  Day:
                 Date:                              Daily#:

Current Events/Special Occasion:

_____

_____

I am so Grateful for:

_____

_____

_____

_____

_____

_____

_____

_____

_____

_____

The Highlight of my day was:

_____

_____

*He is a wise man who does not grieve for the things which he has not, but rejoices for those which he has. ~Epictetus*

# GRATITUDE TOMORROW

GRATITUDE TODAY  Day:
                 Date:                                    Daily#:

Current Events/Special Occasion:

_____

_____

I am so Grateful for:

_____

_____

_____

_____

_____

_____

_____

_____

_____

_____

The Highlight of my day was:

_____

_____

*What a miserable thing life is: you're living in clover, only the clover isn't good enough. ~Bertolt Brecht, Jungle of Cities, 1924*

# GRATITUDE TOMORROW

GRATITUDE TODAY    Day:
                   Date:                                    Daily#:

Current Events/Special Occasion:

_____

_____

I am so Grateful for:

_____

_____

_____

_____

_____

_____

_____

_____

_____

_____

The Highlight of my day was:

_____

_____

*Gratitude is the best attitude. ~Author Unknown*

# GRATITUDE TOMORROW

GRATITUDE TODAY   Day:
                  Date:                                    Daily#:

Current Events/Special Occasion:

_____

_____

I am so Grateful for:

_____

_____

_____

_____

_____

_____

_____

_____

_____

_____

The Highlight of my day was:

_____

_____

*Not what we say about our blessings, but how we use them, is the true measure of our thanksgiving. ~W.T. Purkiser*

# GRATITUDE TOMORROW

GRATITUDE TODAY  Day:
                 Date:                                      Daily#:

Current Events/Special Occasion:

_____

_____

I am so Grateful for:

_____

_____

_____

_____

_____

_____

_____

_____

_____

_____

The Highlight of my day was:

_____

_____

_____

*We thank Thee, O Father of all, for... all the soul-help that sad souls understand. ~Will Carleton*

# GRATITUDE TOMORROW

GRATITUDE TODAY   Day:
                  Date:                                Daily#:

Current Events/Special Occasion:

_____

_____

I am so Grateful for:

_____

_____

_____

_____

_____

_____

_____

_____

_____

_____

The Highlight of my day was:

_____

_____

_____

*We can only be said to be alive in those moments when our hearts are conscious of our treasures. ~Thornton Wilder*

# GRATITUDE TOMORROW

GRATITUDE TODAY   Day:
                  Date:                                Daily#:

Current Events/Special Occasion:

_____

_____

I am so Grateful for:

_____

_____

_____

_____

_____

_____

_____

_____

_____

_____

The Highlight of my day was:

_____

_____

*Gratitude is a quality similar to electricity: it must be produced and discharged and used up in order to exist at all. ~William Faulkner*

# GRATITUDE TOMORROW

GRATITUDE TODAY   Day:
                  Date:                                    Daily#:

Current Events/Special Occasion:

_____

_____

I am so Grateful for:

_____

_____

_____

_____

_____

_____

_____

_____

_____

The Highlight of my day was:

_____

_____

*If you want to turn your life around, try thankfulness. It will change your life mightily. ~Gerald Good*

# GRATITUDE TOMORROW

GRATITUDE TODAY   Day:
                  Date:                          Daily#:

Current Events/Special Occasion:

_____

_____

I am so Grateful for:

_____

_____

_____

_____

_____

_____

_____

_____

_____

_____

The Highlight of my day was:

_____

_____

*Gratitude is the least of the virtues, but ingratitude is the worst of vices.*
*~Thomas Fuller*

# GRATITUDE TOMORROW

GRATITUDE TODAY  Day:
                 Date:                           Daily#:

Current Events/Special Occasion:

_____

_____

I am so Grateful for:

_____

_____

_____

_____

_____

_____

_____

_____

_____

_____

The Highlight of my day was:

_____

_____

*There is not a more pleasing exercise of the mind than gratitude. It is accompanied with such an inward satisfaction that the duty is done. ~Joseph Addison*

# GRATITUDE TOMORROW

GRATITUDE TODAY  Day:
                 Date:                          Daily#:

Current Events/Special Occasion:

_____

_____

I am so Grateful for:

_____

_____

_____

_____

_____

_____

_____

_____

_____

The Highlight of my day was:

_____

_____

_____

*I feel a very unusual sensation - if it is not indigestion, I think it must be gratitude. ~Benjamin Disraeli*

# GRATITUDE TOMORROW

GRATITUDE TODAY   Day:
                  Date:                                    Daily#:

Current Events/Special Occasion:

_____

_____

I am so Grateful for:

_____

_____

_____

_____

_____

_____

_____

_____

_____

_____

The Highlight of my day was:

_____

_____

_____

*There is no greater difference between men than between grateful and ungrateful people. ~R.H. Blyth*

# GRATITUDE TOMORROW

GRATITUDE TODAY  Day:
                 Date:                                    Daily#:

Current Events/Special Occasion:

_____

_____

I am so Grateful for:

_____

_____

_____

_____

_____

_____

_____

_____

_____

_____

The Highlight of my day was:

_____

_____

*Courtesies of a small and trivial character are the ones which strike deepest in the grateful and appreciating heart. ~H Clay*

# GRATITUDE TOMORROW

GRATITUDE TODAY    Day:
                   Date:                                    Daily#:

Current Events/Special Occasion:

_____

_____

I am so Grateful for:

_____

_____

_____

_____

_____

_____

_____

_____

_____

The Highlight of my day was:

_____

_____

*Who does not thank for little will not thank for much. ~Estonian Proverb*

# GRATITUDE TOMORROW

GRATITUDE TODAY  Day:
                 Date:                              Daily#:

Current Events/Special Occasion:

_____

_____

I am so Grateful for:

_____

_____

_____

_____

_____

_____

_____

_____

_____

_____

The Highlight of my day was:

_____

_____

_____

*All that we behold is full of blessings. ~William Wordsworth*

# GRATITUDE TOMORROW

GRATITUDE TODAY  Day:

Date:                                    Daily#:

Current Events/Special Occasion:

_____

_____

I am so Grateful for:

_____

_____

_____

_____

_____

_____

_____

_____

_____

_____

_____

The Highlight of my day was:

_____

_____

*The hardest arithmetic to master is that which The Human enables us to count our blessings. ~Eric Hoffer*

# GRATITUDE TOMORROW

GRATITUDE TODAY   Day:
                  Date:                              Daily#:

Current Events/Special Occasion:

_____

_____

I am so Grateful for:

_____

_____

_____

_____

_____

_____

_____

_____

_____

_____

The Highlight of my day was:

_____

_____

_____

*Gratitude is the fairest blossom which springs from the soul. ~Henry Ward Beecher*

# GRATITUDE TOMORROW

GRATITUDE TODAY   Day:
                  Date:                                    Daily#:

Current Events/Special Occasion:

_____

_____

I am so Grateful for:

_____

_____

_____

_____

_____

_____

_____

_____

_____

_____

The Highlight of my day was:

_____

_____

*When our perils are past, shall our gratitude sleep? ~George Canning*

# GRATITUDE TOMORROW

GRATITUDE TODAY   Day:

                  Date:                                    Daily#:

Current Events/Special Occasion:

_____

_____

I am so Grateful for:

_____

_____

_____

_____

_____

_____

_____

_____

_____

_____

_____

The Highlight of my day was:

_____

_____

*As we express our gratitude, we must never forget that the highest*
*appreciation is not to utter words, but to live by them. ~J. F. Kennedy*

# GRATITUDE TOMORROW

GRATITUDE TODAY   Day:
                  Date:                              Daily#:

Current Events/Special Occasion:

_____

_____

I am so Grateful for:

_____

_____

_____

_____

_____

_____

_____

_____

_____

_____

The Highlight of my day was:

_____

_____

*We often take for granted the very things that most deserve our gratitude.*
*~Cynthia Ozick*

# GRATITUDE TOMORROW

GRATITUDE TODAY   Day:
                  Date:                          Daily#:

Current Events/Special Occasion:

_____

_____

I am so Grateful for:

_____

_____

_____

_____

_____

_____

_____

_____

_____

The Highlight of my day was:

_____

_____

*The grateful person, being still the most severe exacter of himself, not only confesses, but proclaims, his debts. ~R South*

# GRATITUDE TOMORROW

# GRATITUDE TODAY  Day:
### Date:                                    Daily#:

Current Events/Special Occasion:

_____

_____

I am so Grateful for:

_____

_____

_____

_____

_____

_____

_____

_____

_____

The Highlight of my day was:

_____

_____

_____

*Gratitude is merely the secret hope of further favors. ~François Duc de La Rochefoucauld*

# GRATITUDE TOMORROW

GRATITUDE TODAY   Day:
                  Date:                          Daily#:

Current Events/Special Occasion:

_____

_____

I am so Grateful for:

_____

_____

_____

_____

_____

_____

_____

_____

_____

_____

_____

The Highlight of my day was:

_____

_____

*Most human beings have an almost infinite capacity for taking things for granted. ~Aldous Huxley*

# GRATITUDE TOMORROW

GRATITUDE TODAY   Day:
                  Date:                                    Daily#:

Current Events/Special Occasion:

_____

_____

I am so Grateful for:

_____

_____

_____

_____

_____

_____

_____

_____

_____

_____

The Highlight of my day was:

_____

_____

_____

*Hem your blessings with thankfulness so they don't unravel. ~Author Unknown*

# GRATITUDE TOMORROW

GRATITUDE TODAY   Day:
                  Date:                              Daily#:

Current Events/Special Occasion:

_____

_____

I am so Grateful for:

_____

_____

_____

_____

_____

_____

_____

_____

_____

_____

The Highlight of my day was:

_____

_____

_____

*God gave you a gift of 86,400 seconds today. Have you used one to say "thank you?" ~William A. Ward*

# GRATITUDE TOMORROW

GRATITUDE TODAY Day:
Date: Daily#:

Current Events/Special Occasion:

_____

_____

I am so Grateful for:

_____

_____

_____

_____

_____

_____

_____

_____

_____

_____

The Highlight of my day was:

_____

_____

_____

*Gratitude makes sense of our past, brings peace for today, and creates a vision for tomorrow. ~Melody Beattie*

# GRATITUDE TOMORROW

GRATITUDE TODAY   Day:
                  Date:                                    Daily#:

Current Events/Special Occasion:

_____

_____


I am so Grateful for:

_____

_____

_____

_____

_____

_____

_____

_____

_____

_____


The Highlight of my day was:

_____

_____

_____

*I am full of gratitude for my life - and for this house~. J. Clary*

# GRATITUDE TOMORROW

GRATITUDE TODAY   Day:
                  Date:                                    Daily#:

Current Events/Special Occasion:

_____

_____

I am so Grateful for:

_____

_____

_____

_____

_____

_____

_____

_____

_____

_____

The Highlight of my day was:

_____

_____

*Saying thank you is more than good manners. It is good spirituality." -*
*Alfred Painter*

# GRATITUDE TOMORROW

GRATITUDE TODAY  Day:

Date:                                    Daily#:

Current Events/Special Occasion:

_____

_____

I am so Grateful for:

_____

_____

_____

_____

_____

_____

_____

_____

_____

_____

The Highlight of my day was:

_____

_____

_Joy is the simplest form of gratitude. ~ Karl Barth_

# GRATITUDE TOMORROW

GRATITUDE TODAY   Day:
                  Date:                                    Daily#:

Current Events/Special Occasion:

_____

_____

I am so Grateful for:

_____

_____

_____

_____

_____

_____

_____

_____

_____

_____

The Highlight of my day was:

_____

_____

*Nothing is more honorable than a grateful heart. ~Lucius Annaeus Seneca*

# GRATITUDE TOMORROW

GRATITUDE TODAY   Day:
                  Date:                                    Daily#:

Current Events/Special Occasion:

_____

_____

I am so Grateful for:

_____

_____

_____

_____

_____

_____

_____

_____

_____

_____

_____

The Highlight of my day was:

_____

_____

_____

*When we give cheerfully and accept gratefully, everyone is blessed. ~ Maya Angelou*

# GRATITUDE TOMORROW

GRATITUDE TODAY   Day:
                  Date:                              Daily#:

Current Events/Special Occasion:

_____

_____

I am so Grateful for:

_____

_____

_____

_____

_____

_____

_____

_____

_____

_____

The Highlight of my day was:

_____

_____

_____

*Gratitude for the present moment and the fullness of life now is the true prosperity. ~ Eckhart Tolle*

## GRATITUDE TOMORROW

GRATITUDE TODAY   Day:
                    Date:                                        Daily#:

Current Events/Special Occasion:

_____

_____

I am so Grateful for:

_____

_____

_____

_____

_____

_____

_____

_____

_____

_____

The Highlight of my day was:

_____

_____

_____

*The best way to appreciate your job is to imagine yourself without one ~ Oscar Wilde*

# GRATITUDE TOMORROW

GRATITUDE TODAY   Day:

                             Date:                                  Daily#:

Current Events/Special Occasion:

I am so Grateful for:

The Highlight of my day was:

*We tend to forget that happiness doesn't come as a result of getting something we don't have, but rather of recognizing and appreciating what we do have. ~ Frederick Koenig*

# GRATITUDE TOMORROW

GRATITUDE TODAY  Day:

Date:                                        Daily#:

Current Events/Special Occasion:

_____

_____

I am so Grateful for:

_____

_____

_____

_____

_____

_____

_____

_____

_____

_____

The Highlight of my day was:

_____

_____

_____

*The single greatest thing you can do to change your life today would be to start being grateful today~ Oprah Winfrey*

# GRATITUDE TOMORROW

GRATITUDE TODAY   Day:
                  Date:                              Daily#:

Current Events/Special Occasion:

_____

_____

I am so Grateful for:

_____

_____

_____

_____

_____

_____

_____

_____

_____

_____

The Highlight of my day was:

_____

_____

*Silent gratitude isn't much use to anyone. ~G.B. Stern*

# GRATITUDE TOMORROW

GRATITUDE TODAY   Day:
                  Date:                          Daily#:

Current Events/Special Occasion:

_____

_____

I am so Grateful for:

_____

_____

_____

_____

_____

_____

_____

_____

_____

The Highlight of my day was:

_____

_____

*If the only prayer you said in your whole life was, "thank you," that would suffice. ~Meister Eckhart*

# GRATITUDE TOMORROW

GRATITUDE TODAY  Day:
                  Date:                                    Daily#:

Current Events/Special Occasion:

_____

_____

I am so Grateful for:

_____

_____

_____

_____

_____

_____

_____

_____

_____

The Highlight of my day was:

_____

_____

*There is no such thing as gratitude unexpressed. If it is unexpressed, it is plain, old-fashioned ingratitude. ~R.Brault*

# GRATITUDE TOMORROW

GRATITUDE TODAY  Day:

Date:                                    Daily#:

Current Events/Special Occasion:

_____

_____

I am so Grateful for:

_____

_____

_____

_____

_____

_____

_____

_____

_____

_____

The Highlight of my day was:

_____

_____

*Gratitude is the memory of the heart. ~Jean Baptiste Massieu, translated from French*

# GRATITUDE TOMORROW

GRATITUDE TODAY   Day:
                  Date:                              Daily#:

Current Events/Special Occasion:

_____

_____

I am so Grateful for:

_____

_____

_____

_____

_____

_____

_____

_____

_____

_____

The Highlight of my day was:

_____

_____

*When we were children we were grateful to those who filled our stockings at Christmas time. Why are we not grateful? ~G.K.*

# GRATITUDE TOMORROW

GRATITUDE TODAY  Day:
                 Date:                              Daily#:

Current Events/Special Occasion:

_____

_____

I am so Grateful for:

_____

_____

_____

_____

_____

_____

_____

_____

_____

_____

The Highlight of my day was:

_____

_____

_____

*The only people with whom you should try to get even are those who have helped you. ~John E. Southard*

# GRATITUDE TOMORROW

GRATITUDE TODAY  Day:
                 Date:                          Daily#:

Current Events/Special Occasion:

_____

_____

I am so Grateful for:

_____

_____

_____

_____

_____

_____

_____

_____

_____

_____

The Highlight of my day was:

_____

_____

*Gratitude is an art of painting an adversity into a lovely picture. ~Kak Sri*

# GRATITUDE TOMORROW

GRATITUDE TODAY   Day:
                  Date:                        Daily#:

Current Events/Special Occasion:

_____

_____

I am so Grateful for:

_____

_____

_____

_____

_____

_____

_____

_____

_____

_____

The Highlight of my day was:

_____

_____

*If you have lived, take thankfully the past. ~John Dryden*

# GRATITUDE TOMORROW

GRATITUDE TODAY   Day:
                  Date:                                Daily#:

Current Events/Special Occasion:

_____

_____

I am so Grateful for:

_____

_____

_____

_____

_____

_____

_____

_____

_____

_____

The Highlight of my day was:

_____

_____

_____

*As each day comes to us refreshed and anew, so does my gratitude renew itself daily. Terri Gauteet*

# GRATITUDE TOMORROW

GRATITUDE TODAY  Day:
                 Date:                              Daily#:

Current Events/Special Occasion:

_____

_____

I am so Grateful for:

_____

_____

_____

_____

_____

_____

_____

_____

_____

_____

_____

The Highlight of my day was:

_____

_____

*I would maintain that thanks are the highest form of thought; and that gratitude is happiness doubled by wonder. ~G.K.*

# GRATITUDE TOMORROW

# GRATITUDE TODAY   Day:
                    Date:                                    Daily#:

Current Events/Special Occasion:

_____

_____

I am so Grateful for:

_____

_____

_____

_____

_____

_____

_____

_____

_____

_____

The Highlight of my day was:

_____

_____

*Feeling gratitude and not expressing it is like wrapping a present and not giving it. ~William Arthur Ward*

# GRATITUDE TOMORROW

GRATITUDE TODAY  Day:

Date:                                        Daily#:

Current Events/Special Occasion:

_____

_____

I am so Grateful for:

_____

_____

_____

_____

_____

_____

_____

_____

_____

_____

The Highlight of my day was:

_____

_____

_____

*If a fellow isn't thankful for what he's got, he isn't likely to be thankful for what he's going to get. ~Frank A. Clark*

# GRATITUDE TOMORROW

GRATITUDE TODAY  Day:

Date:                                    Daily#:

Current Events/Special Occasion:

_____

_____

I am so Grateful for:

_____

_____

_____

_____

_____

_____

_____

_____

_____

The Highlight of my day was:

_____

_____

_____

*The unthankful heart... discovers no mercies; but the iron, so it will find,*
*heavenly blessings! ~Henry Ward Beec*

# GRATITUDE TOMORROW

GRATITUDE TODAY   Day:
                  Date:                                      Daily#:

Current Events/Special Occasion:

_____

_____

I am so Grateful for:

_____

_____

_____

_____

_____

_____

_____

_____

_____

The Highlight of my day was:

_____

_____

*Grace isn't a little prayer you chant before receiving a meal. It's a way to live. ~Attributed to Jacqueline Winspear*

# GRATITUDE TOMORROW

GRATITUDE TODAY   Day:
                  Date:                                    Daily#:

Current Events/Special Occasion:

_____

_____

I am so Grateful for:

_____

_____

_____

_____

_____

_____

_____

_____

_____

_____

The Highlight of my day was:

_____

_____

*Praise the bridge that carried you over. ~George Colman*

# GRATITUDE TOMORROW

GRATITUDE TODAY   Day:
                  Date:                              Daily#:

Current Events/Special Occasion:

_____

_____

I am so Grateful for:

_____

_____

_____

_____

_____

_____

_____

_____

_____

The Highlight of my day was:

_____

_____

*If you count all your assets, you always show a profit. ~Robert Quillen*

# GRATITUDE TOMORROW

# GRATITUDE TODAY   Day:
### Date:                                              Daily#:

Current Events/Special Occasion:

_____

_____

I am so Grateful for:

_____

_____

_____

_____

_____

_____

_____

_____

_____

The Highlight of my day was:

_____

_____

*He is a wise man who does not grieve for the things which he has not, but rejoices for those which he has. ~Epictetus*

# GRATITUDE TOMORROW

GRATITUDE TODAY  Day:

Date:                                              Daily#:

Current Events/Special Occasion:

_____

_____

I am so Grateful for:

_____

_____

_____

_____

_____

_____

_____

_____

_____

_____

_____

The Highlight of my day was:

_____

_____

_____

*What a miserable thing life is: you're living in clover, only the clover isn't good enough. ~Bertolt Brecht, Jungle of Cities, 1924*

# GRATITUDE TOMORROW

GRATITUDE TODAY   Day:
                 Date:                          Daily#:

Current Events/Special Occasion:

_____

_____

I am so Grateful for:

_____

_____

_____

_____

_____

_____

_____

_____

_____

_____

The Highlight of my day was:

_____

_____

*Gratitude is the best attitude. ~Author Unknown*

# GRATITUDE TOMORROW

GRATITUDE TODAY  Day:
                 Date:                                    Daily#:

Current Events/Special Occasion:

_____

_____

I am so Grateful for:

_____

_____

_____

_____

_____

_____

_____

_____

_____

_____

The Highlight of my day was:

_____

_____

_____

*Not what we say about our blessings, but how we use them, is the true measure of our thanksgiving. ~W.T. Purkiser*

## GRATITUDE TOMORROW

GRATITUDE TODAY   Day:
                  Date:                              Daily#:

Current Events/Special Occasion:

_____

_____

I am so Grateful for:

_____

_____

_____

_____

_____

_____

_____

_____

_____

_____

The Highlight of my day was:

_____

_____

*We thank Thee, O Father of all, for... all the soul-help that sad souls understand. ~Will Carleton*

# GRATITUDE TOMORROW

GRATITUDE TODAY  Day:
                 Date:                                    Daily#:

Current Events/Special Occasion:

_____

_____

I am so Grateful for:

_____

_____

_____

_____

_____

_____

_____

_____

_____

_____

_____

The Highlight of my day was:

_____

_____

*We can only be said to be alive in those moments when our hearts are conscious of our treasures. ~Thornton Wilder*

# GRATITUDE TOMORROW

GRATITUDE TODAY   Day:
                  Date:                                    Daily#:

Current Events/Special Occasion:

_____

_____

I am so Grateful for:

_____

_____

_____

_____

_____

_____

_____

_____

_____

The Highlight of my day was:

_____

_____

_____

*Gratitude is a quality similar to electricity: it must be produced and discharged and used up in order to exist at all. ~William Faulkner*

# GRATITUDE TOMORROW

GRATITUDE TODAY  Day:

Date:                                          Daily#:

Current Events/Special Occasion:

_____

_____

I am so Grateful for:

_____

_____

_____

_____

_____

_____

_____

_____

_____

_____

The Highlight of my day was:

_____

_____

*If you want to turn your life around, try thankfulness. It will change your life mightily. ~Gerald Good*

## GRATITUDE TOMORROW

GRATITUDE TODAY  Day:
                 Date:                                    Daily#:

Current Events/Special Occasion:

_____

_____

I am so Grateful for:

_____

_____

_____

_____

_____

_____

_____

_____

_____

_____

The Highlight of my day was:

_____

_____

*Gratitude is the least of the virtues, but ingratitude is the worst of vices.*
*~Thomas Fuller*

# GRATITUDE TOMORROW

GRATITUDE TODAY   Day:
                          Date:                              Daily#:

Current Events/Special Occasion:

_____

_____

I am so Grateful for:

_____

_____

_____

_____

_____

_____

_____

_____

_____

_____

The Highlight of my day was:

_____

_____

*There is not a more pleasing exercise of the mind than gratitude. It is accompanied with such an inward satisfaction that the duty is done. ~Joseph Addison*

## GRATITUDE TOMORROW

GRATITUDE TODAY   Day:
                  Date:                                    Daily#:

Current Events/Special Occasion:

_____

_____

I am so Grateful for:

_____

_____

_____

_____

_____

_____

_____

_____

_____

_____

The Highlight of my day was:

_____

_____

_____

*I feel a very unusual sensation - if it is not indigestion, I think it must be gratitude. ~Benjamin Disraeli*

# GRATITUDE TOMORROW

GRATITUDE TODAY  Day:

Date:                                                    Daily#:

Current Events/Special Occasion:

_____

_____

I am so Grateful for:

_____

_____

_____

_____

_____

_____

_____

_____

_____

_____

The Highlight of my day was:

_____

_____

_____

*There is no greater difference between men than between grateful and ungrateful people. ~R.H. Blyth*

# GRATITUDE TOMORROW

GRATITUDE TODAY  Day:

Date:                                          Daily#:

Current Events/Special Occasion:

_____

_____

I am so Grateful for:

_____

_____

_____

_____

_____

_____

_____

_____

_____

_____

The Highlight of my day was:

_____

_____

_____

*Courtesies of a small and trivial character are the ones which strike deepest in the grateful and appreciating heart. ~H Clay*

# GRATITUDE TOMORROW

GRATITUDE TODAY   Day:
                  Date:                                    Daily#:

Current Events/Special Occasion:

_____

_____

I am so Grateful for:

_____

_____

_____

_____

_____

_____

_____

_____

_____

_____

The Highlight of my day was:

_____

_____

*Who does not thank for little will not thank for much. ~Estonian Proverb*

# GRATITUDE TOMORROW

GRATITUDE TODAY   Day:
                  Date:                          Daily#:

Current Events/Special Occasion:

_____

_____

I am so Grateful for:

_____

_____

_____

_____

_____

_____

_____

_____

_____

The Highlight of my day was:

_____

_____

*All that we behold is full of blessings. ~William Wordsworth*

# GRATITUDE TOMORROW

GRATITUDE TODAY  Day:
                 Date:                                    Daily#:

Current Events/Special Occasion:

_____

_____

I am so Grateful for:

_____

_____

_____

_____

_____

_____

_____

_____

_____

_____

The Highlight of my day was:

_____

_____

_____

*The hardest arithmetic to master is that which The Human enables us to count our blessings. ~Eric Hoffer*

# GRATITUDE TOMORROW

GRATITUDE TODAY   Day:
                  Date:                          Daily#:

Current Events/Special Occasion:

_____

_____

I am so Grateful for:

_____

_____

_____

_____

_____

_____

_____

_____

_____

_____

_____

The Highlight of my day was:

_____

_____

*Gratitude is the fairest blossom which springs from the soul. ~Henry Ward Beecher*

# GRATITUDE TOMORROW

GRATITUDE TODAY  Day:
                 Date:                                    Daily#:

Current Events/Special Occasion:

_____

_____

I am so Grateful for:

_____

_____

_____

_____

_____

_____

_____

_____

_____

_____

_____

The Highlight of my day was:

_____

_____

*When our perils are past, shall our gratitude sleep? ~George Canning*

# GRATITUDE TOMORROW

# GRATITUDE TODAY   Day:
Date:                                                        Daily#:

Current Events/Special Occasion:

_____

_____

I am so Grateful for:

_____

_____

_____

_____

_____

_____

_____

_____

_____

_____

The Highlight of my day was:

_____

_____

_____

*As we express our gratitude, we must never forget that the highest*
*appreciation is not to utter words, but to live by them. ~J. F. Kennedy*

# GRATITUDE TOMORROW

GRATITUDE TODAY  Day:

Date:                                    Daily#:

Current Events/Special Occasion:

_____

_____

I am so Grateful for:

_____

_____

_____

_____

_____

_____

_____

_____

_____

_____

The Highlight of my day was:

_____

_____

*We often take for granted the very things that most deserve our gratitude.*
*~Cynthia Ozick*

# GRATITUDE TOMORROW

GRATITUDE TODAY   Day:
                  Date:                                            Daily#:

Current Events/Special Occasion:

I am so Grateful for:

The Highlight of my day was:

*The grateful person, being still the most severe exacter of himself, not only confesses, but proclaims, his debts. ~R South*

# GRATITUDE TOMORROW

GRATITUDE TODAY   Day:
                  Date:                                    Daily#:

Current Events/Special Occasion:

_____

_____

I am so Grateful for:

_____

_____

_____

_____

_____

_____

_____

_____

_____

_____

_____

The Highlight of my day was:

_____

_____

_____

*Gratitude is merely the secret hope of further favors. ~François Duc de La Rochefoucauld*

# GRATITUDE TOMORROW

GRATITUDE TODAY   Day:
                                        Date:                                    Daily#:

Current Events/Special Occasion:

_____

_____

I am so Grateful for:

_____

_____

_____

_____

_____

_____

_____

_____

_____

_____

The Highlight of my day was:

_____

_____

*Most human beings have an almost infinite capacity for taking things for granted. ~Aldous Huxley*

# GRATITUDE TOMORROW

GRATITUDE TODAY   Day:
                  Date:                        Daily#:

Current Events/Special Occasion:

_____

_____

I am so Grateful for:

_____

_____

_____

_____

_____

_____

_____

_____

_____

_____

_____

The Highlight of my day was:

_____

_____

_____

*Hem your blessings with thankfulness so they don't unravel. ~Author Unknown*

# GRATITUDE TOMORROW

GRATITUDE TODAY  Day:

Date:                                             Daily#:

Current Events/Special Occasion:

_____

_____

I am so Grateful for:

_____

_____

_____

_____

_____

_____

_____

_____

_____

_____

_____

The Highlight of my day was:

_____

_____

*God gave you a gift of 86,400 seconds today. Have you used one to say*

*"thank you?" ~William A. Ward*

# GRATITUDE TOMORROW

GRATITUDE TODAY   Day:
                  Date:                            Daily#:

Current Events/Special Occasion:

_____

_____

I am so Grateful for:

_____

_____

_____

_____

_____

_____

_____

_____

_____

_____

The Highlight of my day was:

_____

_____

*Gratitude makes sense of our past, brings peace for today, and creates a vision for tomorrow. ~Melody Beattie*

# GRATITUDE TOMORROW

GRATITUDE TODAY  Day:
                 Date:                              Daily#:

Current Events/Special Occasion:

_____

_____

I am so Grateful for:

_____

_____

_____

_____

_____

_____

_____

_____

_____

_____

The Highlight of my day was:

_____

_____

*I am full of gratitude for my life - and for this house~. J. Clary*

# GRATITUDE TOMORROW

## ABOUT THE AUTHOR

David George Brooke, The Brooker – That Gratitude Guy, has been a speaker, teacher, life coach, and best-selling author for over 30 years. He specializes in coaching people to cope and manage the stresses of life by applying an attitude of gratitude. To access his strategies on how to utilize your Daily Gratitude Journal, and to order additional copies, visit his website:

http://www.thebrooker.com

to ?to ?

I I am so sorry about what happend today and I hope you will forgive me. I dont know what I was thinking at the time but I just thought that I did terible so I picked up a ball and kicked it on to the net blocking it from going over, but it hit the top of the net and went over. Also at the time I wanted to win so bad so I said what you could say mean thing at them not thinking before I said it. I just want to say that I am very sorry and I will chang my ways, I promise I will.

45465019R00116

Made in the USA
San Bernardino, CA
09 February 2017